All About Diversity

Contents

4-5 What is diversity?

6-7 Amazing humans

8-9 How are we different?

10-11 What do we wear?

12-13 What can girls and boys do?

14-15 Different bodies

16-17 Different brains

18-19 Understanding each other

20-21 Different kinds of families

22-23 What do we eat?

24-25 Celebrations and festivals

26-27 Show and tell

28-29 What do you like?

30 Some useful diversity words

31 Some notes for grown-ups

Find out what the words in **bold type** mean, and also words in different languages on page 30.

Usborne

All About
Diversity

Felicity Brooks

Illustrated by Mar Ferrero

Designed by Frankie Allen

Diversity consultant:
Dr. Chandrika Devarakonda

What is diversity?

Wouldn't it be boring if people were all the same?

If they wore the same clothes,

ate the same food,

had the same hair,

lived in the same sort of home,

went to the same kind of school,

had the same teacher,

read the same book,

had the same type of family and the same pet,

Blah!

Blah!

said the same thing,

and played exactly the same game every single day?

But luckily our world isn't like that because everyone is DIFFERENT ...

Being different from each other is called DIVERSITY and it is an amazing thing! Which of these two pages do you think looks more interesting?

Amazing humans

Although we're all different, there's one thing that does make us the same. We're all HUMANS and all part of the human race. Humans live all over the world, on six CONTINENTS and in nearly 200 countries.

NORTH AMERICA

EUROPE

Hi! I'm Sophia in Canada. My family came here from Italy.

Hi! I'm Keisha and I'm British. My grandparents came here from Jamaica.

Hello! I'm Jayden in the USA. I'm American.

Hi! I'm Hassan in Spain. My family came from Syria when I was a baby.

Hello! I'm Nadua and I'm Native American.

I'm Moussa in Senegal in the continent of Africa.

There are almost 8 BILLION humans in the world and over 2 BILLION of us are children. People are always moving or having to move around the world. (Some animals do this too.)

I'm Afonso. I live in Brazil and we speak Portuguese.

I'm Osian. My family's from Wales but we live in Peru.

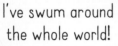

I've swum around the whole world!

SOUTH AMERICA

ANTARCTICA

is far too cold for humans to live here all the time, but there are lots of penguins.

Brrrrrrr

Around the world we . . .

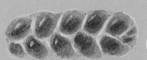 make over 200 types of bread,

 **Ni hao!** **Ciao!** **Dumela!** speak at least 7,000 different languages,

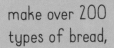 play 1,500 kinds of instruments,

wear over 170 types of hats,

dance over 1,000 sorts of dances.

ASIA
is the biggest continent with more than 40 countries.

No wonder our world is such an interesting place!

Hello! I am Anastasia. in Russia.

Hello! I'm Wang Yong in China.

Hi! I'm Farida. I'm in India.

Hi! I'm Ji-woo. My family's from Korea, but we live in Thailand.

Hello! I'm Angel. I live in Kenya.

I'm Gorata. I'm from Botswana in Africa but now I live in Australia.

AUSTRALIA
is the smallest continent.

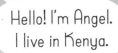 **AFRICA**
is where ALL humans first came from a very very long time ago.

I'm Maia and I'm one of the Māori people who were the first in New Zealand.

Do you know the name of the country you live in? Which continent is it in?

How are we different?

Even in one class at school, the children may be very different. The children in this class have drawn pictures and are talking about themselves. Can you match the drawings with the children?

Our Class

We share things

Our promises

Amira

Ocean

Abeni

Bubbles

First Grade

Lily

Zoe

We listen to each other

Bilal

I got my name from my nana. I've got her pretty hair too!

Abeni's an African name. It means "we asked for her and look, we got her!"

Why do I have so many freckles?

My name's Johanna, but I like to be called Jo.

I love to paint, like my twin, Lily.

We get our skin, eye and hair color from our **birth parents** and **ancestors** (our family who lived long ago). It all depends on something called **melanin**. Everyone has melanin in their skin but some people make more than others and this means their skin is darker. Melanin's job is to stop skin from burning in the sun. If your ancestors lived in a very sunny part of the world, they needed more melanin.

What do YOU look like? Can you draw a picture of yourself? What is YOUR name?

What do we wear?

It's not just our skin, hair and eyes that can make us look different. There can also be A LOT of diversity in what we wear.

Sometimes people need to wear special clothes for work, school or sports, or to dress up for a festival or celebration.

School uniform   Dance clothes   Clothes for special days

Are there any clothes you HAVE to wear? What do you LIKE to wear?
Do you wear any special clothes for special days?

What can girls and boys do?

Some people used to think that girls and boys were very different. They thought that there were some things that only boys or only girls could do, or wear, or play with. But now we know that . . .

Girls can have long or short hair.
Boys can have long or short hair.

Boys can climb.
Girls can climb.

Boys can run. Girls can run.

Boys can wear bright clothes.
Girls can wear bright clothes.

Girls can jump in puddles.
Boys can jump in puddles.

Girls scream and shout.
Boys scream and shout.

Many boys like to dance and sing.
Many girls like to dance and sing.

Some boys don't like to be called boys.
Some girls don't like to be called girls.

Girls' and boys' bodies are a little different, but they can all do the same things.
When these children grow up, who could . . .

be a nurse?	design a bridge?	run a country?
fight a fire?	help sick animals?	fly a plane?
build a house?	be a scientist?	cook a meal?
be a detective?	be an athlete?	take care of a baby?*

What would YOU like to do when you grow up?

* (Answer on page 32)

Different bodies

You may notice some other ways that people's bodies look different on the outside. There are ...

tall people

small people

I'm a little person but I'm a grown-up.

people with lots of hair

people with not much hair

No bus for us!

yap! yap!

people with freckles, rashes, pimples, marks or scars on their skin

It's my birthday today!

85 TODAY

Pleeeease can I try your crutches?

older people

young people

Sorry, NO!

Ooo! The baby's kicking!

pregnant people

Some people look different because they have a disability and use equipment such as a wheelchair to get around.

14

There are lots of different disabilities, and you can't always see that someone has one. There are also different reasons why people have them.

I've been **deaf** since I was born. That means I can't hear. My mom's deaf too.

I'm **blind**. That means I can't see. I lost my sight two years ago.

My job is to help her get to work (so please don't pet me when I'm working!)

Some people have had a disability ever since they were born.

Some people have a disability because of an illness or a health problem.

Huff, puff... I lost my leg in a car accident.

Huff, puff...now I have a prosthetic leg to help me run.

Wow!

Some people have a disability because of an accident.

Someone who has a **learning disability** may need more time or extra help to learn or do some things.

Like everyone, someone with a disability might need a bit of extra help sometimes. Because you can't always see a disability, it's important to try to be kind, patient and friendly with everyone.

Different brains

The way that people's brains work, the way that they think, learn and behave can also be very different. This type of diversity is called NEURODIVERSITY (say "new-ro-die-ver-city").

Someone who's shy might find it hard to talk to people. It doesn't mean they're unfriendly.

> I'm talking a lot inside my head.

Someone who's outgoing finds talking easy and likes meeting people.

Hi!

Anya's Oxygen

> Hi! My name's Sanjay and I'm five and three-quarters and I LOVE marshmallows and I have two sisters and...

> Can anyone see Milly?

Someone with **dyspraxia** might not have very good balance, but be very good at noticing how other people are feeling.

Someone with **dysgraphia** might need extra help with writing, but be very observant.

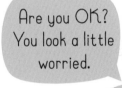

> Are you OK? You look a little worried.

> Oh no! I've lost my pen again.

> It's OK, Josh. It's just behind the books.

SIGH!

> Milly's under the table, Mr. Jonty.

Someone with **dyscalculia** might need extra help with numbers, but may be fantastic with words.

> I've written a poem about the zoo!

The Zoo
There's lots to do when you go to the zoo.
You can see big cats and beautiful bats.
I love going to the zoo!
by Iqbal Zephaniah

Someone on the **autism spectrum** might know a lot about one thing. They might have an amazing memory and be able to concentrate for a long time.

> Tell me all about your coins, Freya.

> I have 207 coins. The oldest is from 1827. It's a penny made of copper.

> This is Britannia with her right hand on a shield, and a trident in her left hand.

Someone with **dyslexia** might need extra help with reading, but may be creative and good at solving problems.

TAP
TAP
TAP

> I don't want to join in.

Someone with **ADHD** might find it hard to sit down and concentrate, but could be full of ideas, creative, sporty and brilliant at remembering facts.

> Oh, this paper looks like a dinosaur!

> Did you know a stegosaurus had 17 plates called scutes on its back?

> ARGH! What's that tapping noise?

> Hmm ... I wonder what's for lunch?

Understanding each other

Everyone needs to communicate (share information) with others, but there's a lot of diversity in the way we do this. Many people communicate by speaking in the language or languages they learned at home.

Tiny babies can't talk, but may start to learn any language by listening to the people around them.

If their caregivers or parents speak different languages, they may learn two, or even more.

When they go to school, or if they move to another country, they may need to learn a new language as well.

As well as speaking different languages, people speak in different ways. Sometimes speaking (and understanding) can be hard work, maybe because . . .

. . . someone gets stuck, or repeats sounds or words. This is called **stammering**.

. . . someone is learning a language and doesn't know all the words yet.

. . . someone has a disability which makes speaking more difficult or slower.

LISTENING carefully and being PATIENT can really help when someone is working hard to speak. Luckily there are many other ways of communicating as well as speaking a language. You might use . . .

a pencil and paper,

pictures and symbols,

your face and body,

GASP CLAP
GIGGLE
SCREAM!

noises and sounds,

happy

flashcards,

a computer, tablet or keyboard communication device,

Anna is signing the word "play."

a sign language such as **makaton**, or **ASL** (American Sign Language) which many deaf people use,

jingle bells,
jingle bells

a song and a dance,

HA,
HA,
HA!

or a secret sign language.

How do you communicate? Do you use any equipment to help your communication? Maybe you speak one language at home and a different one with your friends?

Different kinds of families

Families can be very big or just two people and everything in between. And there are many, many different kinds. Here are just a few...

Some families include parents who have married in a ceremony. Others include parents who are not married.

In **kinship care families**, children live with their grandparents, an aunt, an uncle or a grown-up brother or sister.

A **foster family** looks after children if their **birth family** isn't able to. This can be for a short time or a long time.

In a single parent family, a mom or a dad takes care of the children for most or all of the time.

If you are **adopted**, a new family was found for you because your **birth parents** couldn't take care of you.

Who do you live with? What size and shape is your family?
Do you have any brothers and sisters, or are you an only child?

The kinds of places where families live are very diverse, too. Do you live in any of these?

A brick house

A stilt house

An apartment

A handmade house

A log cabin

A houseboat

A mobile home

A tent

A rondavel

And how do you and your family travel around? Maybe it's by . . .

auto rickshaw, tuk-tuk or taxi,

tandem or bicycle,

BEEP BEEP!

bus,

. . . or on foot?

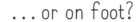

What do we eat?

Everybody needs to eat, but what and how we eat can be very different country to country, family to family and person to person.

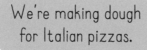
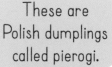

Do you have any special family meals or recipes?

Do you eat any of your food with chopsticks?

Or do you use your right hand?

Maybe you use a spoon, or a knife and fork?

Some people don't eat some kinds of food because of their beliefs or choices. Others are allergic to a type of food and would become sick if they ate it.

People get their food in different ways, too. Around the world many grow, catch or farm food. Many others buy it. How do you get yours?

From a supermarket or a grocery store?

From a garden, a field, a river, a lake or the sea?

From a street market or a farm shop?

From a van or truck?

From a foodbank?

From nature?

My FAVORITES are jollof rice, fried plantain, camembert cheese, cheese scones, paella, mushroom tagliatelle, tarka dhal, bao buns, battered squid, cantaloupe melon, injera flatbread, pumpkin pie, crispy seaweed, couscous, sushi, fried chicken and ice cream. (But NOT altogether!)

Do you have a favorite food or favorite meal?
Have you ever tried something new and really liked it?

Celebrations and festivals

Through the year there are so many different festivals, things to celebrate and different ways of celebrating. Celebrations might include . . .

Happy Birthday!

fireworks for Diwali

a special cake, a song and presents for birthdays

Merry Christmas!

a parade through the streets with a huge dragon for Chinese New Year

a feast, presents and greetings for Christmas

Eid Mubarak!

Happy New Year everybody!

Follow me!

a feast, presents and greetings for Eid al-Fitr

ooooooo ahhhhhh!

special candles and doughnuts for Hanukkah

scary costumes for Halloween

Which festivals do you and your family celebrate?
Maybe you go to a **temple**, a **synagogue**, a **church**,
a **mosque**, a **shrine** or a **gurdwara** for a religious festival?
Do you wear any special clothes or eat special foods?

Show and tell

These children are showing and talking about things that are special to their families or in their **culture** (find out what this means on page 30).

My mom tells us these stories about Tikoulou from Mauritius.

This is a Filipino song that my Lolo sings with me, in Tagalog and English.

Paa, tuhod, balikat, ulo

Toes, knees, shoulders, head

rarrr rarrr

My dad wore this lion mask for festivals in India when he was little.

This is my mom's shadow puppet. It's the only thing she has from Indonesia.

These are pictures of all the places my family has lived. We move a lot!

This is my uncle's oud. He's taught lots of people how to play it.

This is my nana's elephant collection. She says they bring good luck!

We are showing namaste, a respectful way to greet people.

hop! hop!

This is the costume I wear for Irish dancing.

This is my Baba. She is wearing her special costume from Ukraine.

This game is called mancala. People have played it in Egypt for thousands of years.

This is my mom when she was the May Queen and danced around a maypole.

You can show old or new things at a show and tell. Some children show things to do with their family's beliefs, or things that they hope will bring them luck.

My dad's lucky football hat – it doesn't always work!

The Hand of Fatima helps protect us.

Our Fortune Cat brings good luck.

Here's my lucky Barcelos Rooster from Portugal.

What would you talk about or show to your friends?
Do you have something that's special to you and your family?

What do you like?

Some more things that make us all different and make each of us **unique** is what we like, what we don't like, and what we can do.

But although we are all different, and each one of us is unique and special, there are things that EVERYONE could do to help us ALL live, play and work together in a fair way. These children have some ideas . . .

We can be KIND to each other.

We can LISTEN to each other.

We can RESPECT each other's differences.

We can all be POLITE to each other.

We can INCLUDE everybody in our games.

We can HELP each other.

We can SHARE and TAKE TURNS.

We can SPEAK UP when someone is being mean.

We can be PROUD of ourselves and our families.

Do you have any more great ideas to help make our amazing, diverse world an even better place?

Some useful diversity words

ADHD or Attention Deficit Hyperactivity Disorder – a type of neurodiversity that may affect people's behavior, thinking and learning

Adopted – If a child is adopted, a new family was found for them because their birth parents were not able to take care of them.

Ancestors – relatives who lived long ago

ASL or American Sign Language – a way of communicating using gestures, facial expressions, and body language

Autism spectrum – If someone is on the autism spectrum, they have a form of neurodiversity that may affect their behavior and communication.

Birth family/Birth parents – the family/parents someone had when they were born

Blind – Someone who is blind has a disability that causes them to be unable to see.

Chinese New Year – a yearly festival that celebrates the start of a new year on the traditional Chinese calendar

Christmas – a yearly festival that celebrates the birth of Jesus Christ in the Christian religion

Church – a place where Christians go to worship

Culture – all the activities, ideas, beliefs, music, poetry, dances, festivals, customs, traditions, and so on that are shared by a group of people

Deaf – Someone who is deaf has a disability that makes them unable to hear.

Diwali – a festival of lights celebrated by Hindus, Jains and Sikhs every year

Dyscalculia, Dysgraphia, Dyslexia and Dyspraxia are all different types of neurodiversity that may affect people's learning, thinking and behavior.

Eid al-Fitr – a religious holiday celebrated by Muslims. It marks the end of the month of Ramadan when many Muslims fast (eat nothing) from sunrise until sunset.

Foster family – a family that looks after children if the children's birth family isn't able to

Gurdwara – a place where Sikhs go to meet and worship

Halloween – the day of October 31st where some children dress up in costumes

Hanukkah – a yearly festival of lights celebrated by Jewish families

Holi – a popular yearly Hindu festival, also known as the festival of spring, the festival of colors and the festival of love

Kabaddi – a team game especially popular in Pakistan and India

Kinship care family – a family where an aunt or grandparent (for example) takes care of the children

Learning disability – If someone has a learning disability, it is harder and takes more time for them to learn certain skills. Learning disabilities vary a lot from person to person.

Makaton – a language program that uses signs, together with speech and symbols, to help people to communicate

Melanin – a natural brown substance in the hair, skin and eyes of people and animals. People's skin color mostly depends on the type and amount of melanin their bodies make.

Mosque – a place where Muslims go to meet and worship

Neurodiversity – the differences in people's brains that mean people behave, think, communicate and learn in different ways

Prosthesis (or "prosthetic") – a specially made body part that someone may sometimes wear because their body is shaped differently at birth, or after an accident or health problem

Stammering (also known as stuttering) – a form of neurodiversity that may affect someone's way of talking

Synagogue – a Jewish temple where people go to meet, worship and study

Temple – a building where people go to worship a god, or gods and goddesses

Unique – not the same as anyone or anything else

Ways to say "hello"
Ciao! – in Italian
Dumela! – in Botswana, Lesotho and some other countries of Southern Africa
Hola! – in Spanish
Ni Hao! – in Mandarin Chinese

Caramba! – an exclamation of surprise in Spanish and Portuguese

Baba – "Grandma" in many languages such as Bulgarian, Russian, Czech and Polish

Lolo – "Grandpa" in Tagalog, a language of the Philippines

Eid Mubarak – a way to wish people a blessed Eid al-Fitr festival

Kung Hei Fat Choy! – one way to wish people good fortune in the Chinese New Year in Cantonese Chinese

Kodomo no Hi – the Children's Festival in Japan

Some notes for grown-ups

Promoting inclusion and diversity matters because we all want **equality of opportunity** for our children, and for all children to be the best they can be. We need to **acknowledge difference** to be able to recognize the support that different people may need. If we ignore someone's skin color, for example, we are ignoring the experiences that have made them who they are. Understanding and celebrating (not just "tolerating") differences of all kinds helps **build children's self-esteem**, makes them feel they belong, and promotes a fairer and more equal society, which in turn **supports all children's development, education and wellbeing.**

The aim of this book is to **be part of that celebration:** to help all children to **feel valued and respected,** and to help them learn to **respond in a kind and fair way** to everyone, regardless of shape, size, age, ability, gender, skin color, nationality, beliefs, language, culture, family background, and so on. Learning to appreciate and celebrate differences is an important skill. So what can you do to help your child develop it?

Talk about diversity and answer questions

We know that babies as young as six months old can recognize differences in the faces of their caregivers, and that by the time they're two, children begin to notice skin color and gender differences. So it's **natural to be curious and notice differences** and it's **good to talk about them.** Chat about diversity with your child from a young age — explain how everyone is different and that's a **positive thing;** it's good to have some things in common with your friends, but also to **respect differences.** If children ask **tricky questions,** try to answer them as openly and accurately as you can using language that you know your child can understand. You can then build on this knowledge as they get older. If your child does say **something discriminatory,** don't overreact, but don't ignore it either. The key is to **respond in a non-judgemental** way using phrases such as: "Let's talk about that for a minute..." or "What do you think made you say that?"

Be a good role model

Your child's **most important role model is you,** and if you want your children to grow up to be kind and empathetic, you can't show tolerance for ageism, sexism, racism, and so on yourself. If someone makes a rude or inappropriate comment, your child needs to see you **speak up to counteract prejudice and stereotyping** when it occurs. Using someone's skin color, religion, gender, culture, appearance, nationality, sexuality, age, language or family background as an insult or as part of a **"joke" can have a profound effect.** Allowing or joining in with "jokes" or "banter" at someone's expense creates a society where that behavior is seen as acceptable and may pave the way for ridicule, name calling, bullying, exclusion and even more serious forms of discrimination.

Be careful with words

It isn't that hard to change the words we use, especially when we know **certain words and phrases can be extremely harmful to individuals** and also shape society's perception of certain groups. **People should not be defined by their differences or disabilities,** so, for example, talk about someone being "on the autism spectrum" rather than being "autistic"; "people who have disabilities" not "the disabled", and remember that a child who has parents with different skin colors or parents with the same skin color but different nationalities is of "mixed heritage." Children learn words from friends and the people around them, so if you hear your child using an offensive, derogatory or outdated term, pick up on it quickly and **explain that the term is rude or unkind.**

Emphasize positives

Encourage children to **look for positives** in themselves and in others. For example, if your child goes to school with a child who uses a mobility aid, they might point out that "Lily can't walk very well." This is a chance to ask, "What's Lily good at?" and find out that Lily is great at chess and drawing. It's important that your child learns to see what Lily **can** do rather than what she **can't.** You might also use the opportunity to **encourage your child to be helpful to others** (in a respectful way) with the things that are difficult for them. You could remind your children that when they have difficulties, it makes them feel good when others offer to help.

Encourage empathy and kindness

The ability to imagine how other people are feeling is an important skill for your child to develop. **Reading all kinds of stories with diverse characters,** and talking about what the characters might be feeling, is a very good way to build empathy. You also need to **be a good role model** here. When you have respectful relationships and interact with others in a kind and caring way, your child learns from your example.

Tackling bullying

It's a sad fact that children who behave differently or look different in some way from their peers still all too easily become targets for bullying, especially as they get older. When talking to your child about differences, it's important to address why **hurting another person's feelings on purpose is always wrong.** If your child hurts another child's feelings, **teach them to apologize.** Ask them how they'd feel if someone said or did something similar to them. Help them to understand that **all people have feelings and all people deserve to be treated with kindness and respect.**

Answer to quiz on page 13: THEY ALL COULD

Usborne Quicklinks

Visit Usborne Quicklinks for links to websites with fun activities that help promote diversity, and video clips to share with children. There is also helpful advice about what to do if you think your child is being bullied or is bullying others.

Go to usborne.com/Quicklinks and type in the keywords "all about diversity." Children should be supervised online. Please read our internet safety guidelines at Usborne Quicklinks.